MAD JACK
BOOKS

CARD TRICKS

Written by Peter Eldin
Illustrated by Dave King

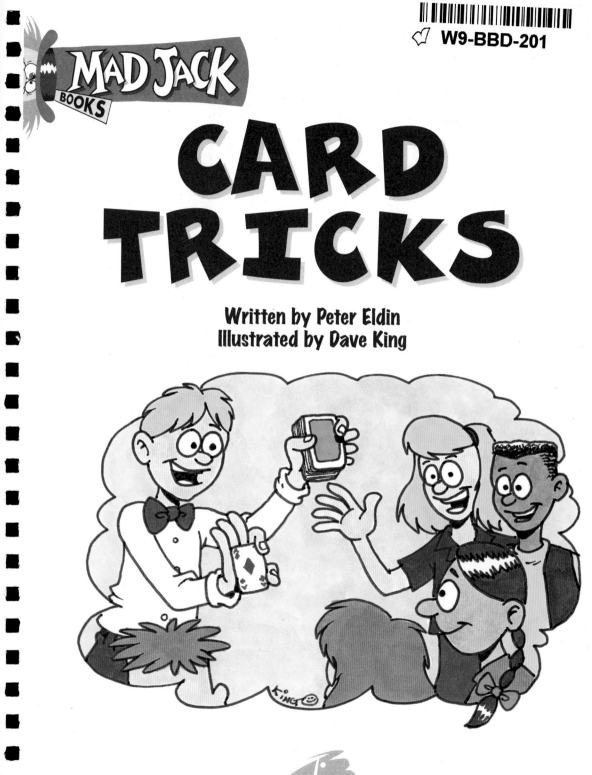

HENDERSON

An imprint of DK Publishing, Inc.

CONTENTS

Conjuring with cards is a fascinating hobby; it's fun to entertain people with magic. It is also satisfying when your otherwise know-it-all brother is completely flummoxed by one of your cunning card tricks. Total humiliation, however, is best avoided if you want to win friends and influence people. (If you have no friends, then, by all means, pursue the humiliation route.) Bottom line — don't let it go to your head — no one likes a smarty pants.

Another thing to avoid is Boring Your Audience. *Just* because there are oodles of tricks in this book does NOT mean that you have to perform every single one of them for your generous audience. They are humoring you and won't do so for more than a socially polite fifteen minutes. More than likely your mother has bribed half of them with milk and cookies and those sort of bribes don't stretch beyond twenty minutes. Assess your audience carefully (check if anyone's chewing). So, if your friends ask you to perform some magic, perform a reasonable selection of tricks — not ALL of them.

Finally, DO make the effort to read all the way through each trick before you attempt to perform it. When you understand what the trick is about, try it out in private. One of the rules for successful conjuring is practice. Don't reveal how a trick is done (no matter how much money they offer). And don't simply read how a trick is done and then think you can do it. You have to practice it first — even if it seems to work itself.

So, give your cards a shuffle and let's take a peek into the wonderful world of card conjuring.

3

MIRACLE CARD

Your Mad Jack card pack is also a Miracle Pack. *No kidding!* It looks like a straight 52 card deck and you can use it for most of the tricks in your book, but — here comes the miracle — the backs are secretly marked. Ask a spectator to freely choose a card, then you, the Magician, can instantly tell what the card is without looking at the card face. Impressed? Take a closer look.

The markings appear in the top left, and bottom right corners, in the first four rows of small circles with the center spot. Learn these positions, then memorize the markings. This card is the two of hearts

HEAR, HEAR

Shuffle the pack several times, then ask a spectator to choose any card from the pack and remember it. (At which point, you glance at the back of the chosen card, secretly reading its markings.) Now ask your spectator to place his card back into the pack. Shuffle the pack, then bring it to your ear, claiming that you are "listening to the pack" and that it has "revealed the chosen card!" Astound the audience as you name the card.

You can vary this trick by "feeling" the pack to find out the identity of the chosen card. Or, keep it simple and just claim that you can "identify any card in the pack without even looking at the face of the cards." Impressive stuff!

CLIPPED

1. Glue five old playing cards together. The cards should be overlapping one another (as shown in fig. 1). The center card should be prominent, either a picture card, an ace, or perhaps one red card among five blacks.

2. Show the glued cards and then turn them face down.

3. Hand a spectator a paper clip with the request that he place it on the king (or whatever the center card is).

4. When the glued card is turned over, the clip is seen to be nowhere near the center card.

This trick works reliably but you should still try it out in private before showing it to anyone.

5

1. Before showing this trick, you must secretly hide the Ace of Diamonds. Put it in a pocket, under a tablecloth, or in a book, for example.

2. Show the audience the other three aces (fig. 1). What the people watching do not know is that the center ace is the Ace of Hearts but, because it is upside down and behind the other two cards, it looks like the Ace of Diamonds.

3. Turn the three cards face down and push each one into the pack as you say "Ace of Clubs, Ace of Diamonds, and the Ace of Spades."

4. You now say some magic words to make the Ace of Diamonds "vanish!" Ask someone to look through the cards and, sure enough, the Ace of Diamonds is nowhere to be seen!

5. Now go to the hiding place and take out the Ace. It looks as if you have transported it there by magic.

FAMILY GET TOGETHER

1. Take the four kings and two other cards from the pack. Hold the six cards so they look like the four kings. The two extra cards are hidden behind your second king. The audience must not be aware of these two hidden cards.

2. Close the fan of cards and place them on the top of the pack. Lift off the first card and let everyone see that it is a king as you place it on the bottom of the pack. Take the second card (without showing it) and push it into the center of the pack. Do the same with the third card. Show the fourth card as a king and place it back on the top of the pack.

4. You now say that "although the kings are now spread throughout the pack, they do like to get together for their little family gatherings."

5. Spread the cards out face up and show that all the kings have come together again.

3. Cut the cards and complete the cut (read how to do this on page 20).

7

ROYAL

1. Take the kings and queens (eight cards) from the pack. It doesn't matter how these are mixed but you must make sure that the suits of the second four match the suits of the first four (so if the first four cards are diamonds, hearts, clubs, spades then the second four must also be diamonds, hearts, clubs, spades). Return these eight cards to the top of the pack.

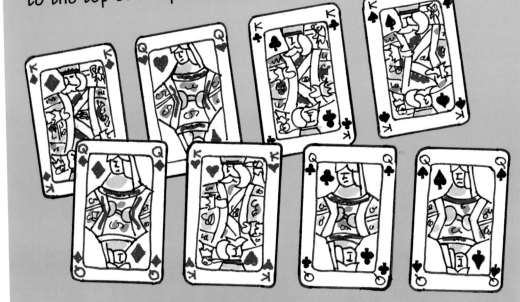

2. Cut (DON'T shuffle) the cards several times to give the appearance that they are being mixed up, but really the royals remain on the top of the pack.

PARTNERS

3. Place the cards behind your back and secretly take off the top four cards and hold them between the first and second fingers (the remaining cards are held by the first finger and thumb). Now you have two piles — a large one and a small one.

4. Take one card from each pile and throw it onto the table — it will be a king and a queen of matching suit. Do exactly the same with the next three cards of each pile.

9

SEPARATE PARTIES

1. This trick continues from the last one. Pick up all the cards. As you do this, make sure that each king is under its matching queen. Some will already be in this position. Those that are not can be easily moved as you pick them up.

2. Place all eight cards behind your back. Hold the cards in your left hand and push the top card between the thumb and forefinger of the right hand. The next card is pushed between the first and second fingers of the right hand. The third card goes between thumb and forefinger, the fourth between first and second fingers and so on.

3. Bring the two groups of cards out and throw them on the table. Would you believe it...you have managed to separate the kings from the queens — one group contains all the queens, the other contains all the kings!

FIND THE LADY

Four aces and a queen are sealed in envelopes. Despite the fact that the five envelopes are thoroughly mixed, you can easily tell which one contains the queen.

The secret is, of course, splendidly simple, as are all the best secrets in magic. When you place the cards in the envelopes, you put each ace in horizontally. The queen, when placed into her envelope, is secretly moved into a vertical position.

1. A member of your audience mixes the envelopes and hands them to you one at a time. You will be able to detect, by touch, the instant you receive the "queen envelope."

2. Tear open this envelope and remove the queen, turning her to a horizontal position in the process, and display her to your now-astounded audience.

GAMBLER'S ACES

Even though a pack is thoroughly shuffled, you are able to find the four aces from it with the cards held behind your back.

1. To do this trick you need to make a small gimmick (the name magicians give to a secret piece of apparatus). This particular gimmick consists of a safety pin attached to a paper clip. Before your performance, secretly pin this to the inside of the back of your jacket. It should be about three inches (8cm) from the bottom of the jacket.

2. Take the four aces from the pack and push them into the secret paper clip. You are now ready to perform the trick.

4. Hold the pack behind your back and bring out the aces, one by one.

3. Have the cards shuffled by one of your spectators. Take the cards back and tell everyone that you will demonstrate how gamblers are able to find the aces even though a pack is thoroughly shuffled.

Everyone will assume they have come from the pack but all you have had to do is pull them from the clip.

1. The pack is shuffled by a volunteer from the audience and then returned to its box.

2. You now pluck the cards from the box one by one — but you call out the name of the card before you take it from the box.

3. What the audience does **NOT** see is that there is a small opening cut in the bottom corner of the box. Through this you can see the details of each card before you remove it.

13

The way that this trick is done is one of the inner secrets of magic. Magicians have kept this secret for many, many years so it is important that you do not reveal how it is done (actually that is true of all the tricks in this book — once you reveal how a trick is done, the mystery is lost, so keep the secrets to yourself).

You do not go anywhere near the pack and yet you are able to say at which card the knife has been placed.

In fact (surprise, surprise), you do go near the pack, but the spectators will forget this when they tell other people about the trick.

1. A pack is shuffled and placed on the table. You then ask someone to slide the blade of a butter knife anywhere into the pack.

2. When the knife has been inserted, you touch the pack to straighten it up, asking your volunteer: "Have you placed the knife exactly where you'd like?" As you ask this, you twist the knife slightly with your left hand and the right lifts the top half of the pack a little.

If you look down quickly, you will see a reflection of the card on the knife blade. With practice it will take you just a second to do this.

3. You now move away from the table as you say: "I do not want to be anywhere near the cards." Strangely enough, people will remember this and will state later that you never touched the cards!

4. You now pretend to concentrate and then you name the card you saw. Someone is asked to open the pack where the knife has been inserted and, sure enough, the card next to the blade is the one you named!

1. Secretly place the Eight of Clubs on the top of the pack and the Nine of Spades on the bottom. Obviously, do not let anyone see you make this advance preparation!

2. When the time comes to show a trick, go through the pack and take out the Nine of Clubs and the Eight of Spades. Show the two cards together and say you are going to do a trick "with these two cards." Do not say what the cards are.

3. Hold the pack, face down, and push the two cards, one at a time, into different parts of the pack.

4. You now say you are going to use your super-sensitive magic fingers to find the two cards. Keep a reasonably tight hold of the pack as you flick your hand into the air. All the cards except the top and bottom one will fly into the air. The top and bottom cards will remain between your finger and thumb. Try to give the impression that you stabbed into the falling cards and grabbed these two from the pack.

5. Show the two cards as if they were the two you showed at the beginning. They are not, of course, the same, but this will not be noticed.

16

MIDAIR

1. You show a pack of cards held in a rubber band. The face card of the pack is the Ace of Hearts but, when you throw the pack into the air and catch it again, the face card is a black card!

2. The secret is in the way the elastic band is around the cards. First, place the band around the pack (fig. 1).

3. Now give the top half of the pack a complete turn (fig. 2).

4. Next you lift up the top half, like opening a book, and fold it over to the other side of the pack.

5. Square the pack up and you are now ready to show it to the audience. You must hold the pack fairly tightly at this stage.

6. Show the face card and then throw the pack into the air and catch it. While it is in the air, the band unwinds and the face card of the pack is "magically" changed!

17

MAD JACK CARD PACK

You may have noticed that your Mad Jack Miracle Cards are ever-so-slightly tapered. Hmm... suspicious? It most certainly is!

Take one card from the pack, turn it end to end, then replace it back in the pack. Now slide your fingers up the sides of the pack — notice anything sticking out? It's a miracle — it's your chosen card! The beauty of this trick is that this slight protrusion is completely invisible to your audience. Test the cards out for yourself a couple of times before you attempt the actual tricks.

Trick Card

Invite a spectator to freely choose a card from the pack.

Ask them to remember the suit and number. Take the chosen card (face down, of course). Discreetly turn the card end to end and return it to the pack. Shuffle the cards. In doing so, you will probably feel the chosen card sticking out. To locate it exactly, run your fingers up the sides of the pack.

Once you get the feel of the tapered cards, try the tricks on page 36.

18

OVERHAND SHUFFLE

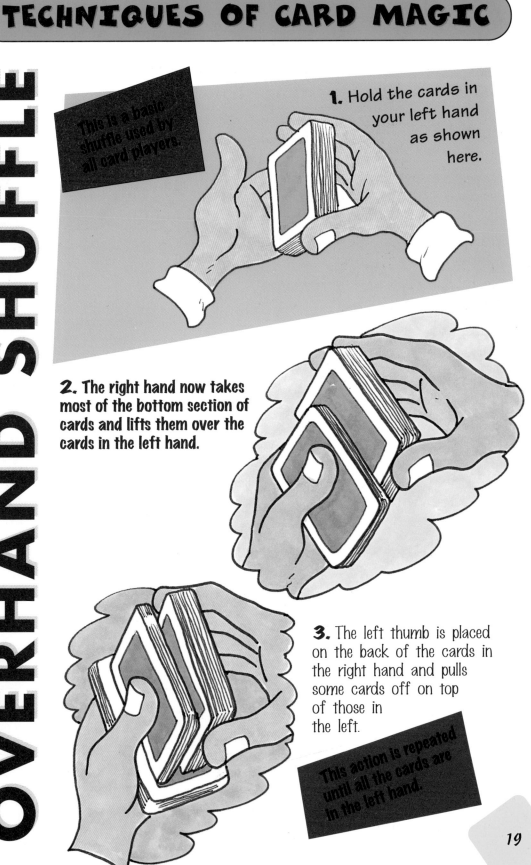

This is a basic shuffle used by all card players.

1. Hold the cards in your left hand as shown here.

2. The right hand now takes most of the bottom section of cards and lifts them over the cards in the left hand.

3. The left thumb is placed on the back of the cards in the right hand and pulls some cards off on top of those in the left.

This action is repeated until all the cards are in the left hand.

CUT THE CARDS

1. To cut the cards, lift off about half the pack and place it to the right.

2. If you now take what was the bottom half and place it on the cards to the right you have "completed the cut."

TAKE A CARD

It is always useful to be able to make someone take the card you want them to take even though you apparently give them a free choice. Magicians call this "forcing."

There are plenty of ways to force a card (shout at it, for starters). Let's start with a simple one:

1. Give the pack a shuffle and, while you are doing this, tilt the cards in your hand so you can see the bottom card when the shuffle is finished. Remember that card.

2. Hold the pack behind your back and turn around so your back is toward the audience. Ask someone to remove a few cards from the top of the pack. When he has taken some, turn back around "to see if he has taken enough." As you do so, secretly move the bottom (remembered) card from the bottom to the top of the pack you still hold.

3. Say "Yes, that will be fine" (as you return the cards to the bottom of the pack) "please take the next card." As you say this, you turn away from the audience again to allow the spectator to take the top card (the one you remembered earlier).

Everyone will think that the chosen card is a free choice but, in fact, it has been forced.

4. The card can now be returned to the pack and the pack shuffled. You can then reveal the card by pretending to read the spectator's mind, or in some other spectacular manner.

This is really sneaky and you need some nerve to carry it off — but, then, that is actually true of all magic. Shrinking violets exit stage left, please.

1. Position the card you want to force on top of the pack. If you wish, you can give the cards a shuffle, controlling the top card to the bottom and then back to the top again as described on page 25.

2. Place the cards on the table and ask a spectator to cut the cards in half.

3. You now pick up the bottom half of the pack and place it across the top half "to mark the cut."

22

4. You must now say something to the spectator like: "I want to show you a really amazing piece of magic." This babble is designed to make the poor spectator forget exactly what has happened, because the next move is *really* sneaky.

5. You now lift off the top half of the pack and point to the top card of the bottom half as you say: "Will you please see what card you cut to?"

It appears that you have allowed the spectator a fair choice but, in fact, the card you are pointing to is the card that was originally on top of the pack – your force card!

SHUFFLE

1. Shuffle the cards and then fan them out for someone to take one. Ask them to remember the card then place it back on the top of the pack.

2. As soon as the card is returned, you give the pack a good shuffle.

Believe it or not, although the cards have been shuffled, you know exactly where the chosen card is – it is the top card of the pack.

3. This means that you could now get someone else to choose a card and they choose exactly the same card as the first person. All you have to do is force the top card, as explained on page 21. But how do you get the chosen card to the top in the first place?

24

4. This is how:

When the chosen card is replaced on the pack, you give the pack an overhand shuffle (see page 19). However, when you start to shuffle, your right hand removes all the cards except the top one (the chosen card). All the rest of the cards are then shuffled on top of the first card so it is now at the bottom of the pack.

5. Give another overhand shuffle but this time keep shuffling until you have only one card (the chosen card) in your right hand, which is simply dropped back on top of the pack.

25

Every magician should know how to find a chosen card that has been returned to the pack. Here is one way to do it:

1. Have the cards shuffled by a volunteer. Quickly fan the cards face up to show your audience that the cards really are mixed up. While you are doing this, secretly remember the bottom card of the pack. This is your "key" card.

2. Turn the cards face down again and spread them out so a member of your audience can select one.

C A R D

3. Ask that person to remember their selected card and to return it to the top of the pack. As soon as the card is on the top, cut the pack so it is lost somewhere in the middle. Cut the cards a few more times.

4. You now scan through the cards as quickly as you can and triumphantly toss one card face down on the table. Ask the spectator to name their chosen card and then turn over the card on the table — it is his card!

You, of course, know which card to throw out because it is the one next to the one you secretly noted at the start of the trick.

ONE FROM THREE

This is a way of getting a spectator to pick an item you want them to pick while apparently giving them a free choice.

1. Cut the pack into three equal piles. Mentally name the piles A, B, and C.

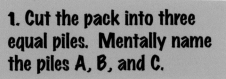

2. For this example, it will be assumed that you want the spectator to pick pile C. Ask your spectator to put his right and left hands on two of the piles.

3a. If he touches A and B, keep talking as you say: "...and push them toward me." That leaves him with pile C (an apparently "free choice").

3b. If he touches A and C (or B and C), simply pick up the rejected pile and put it to one side. Now tell him to push one of the two remaining piles to one side. If pile C is pushed to one side, simply pick up the other pile and put it on top of the first one that was "rejected." Which leaves him with C.

3c. If he pushes pile A/B to one side — perfect! Simply pick up this second, "rejected" pile and put it on the first one that was rejected — leaving him with pile C.

So, whatever the spectator does, you adjust your actions accordingly so he is always left with pile C.

This is a very useful force to know as it can be done with any set of objects.

FALSE CUT

With this crafty technique you appear to give the cards a genuine cut, but in fact all the cards remain in the same order. This is very useful if you have any or all of the cards in a prearranged order for a trick.

1. To help you follow the moves, the top half of the pack has been marked A and the bottom half marked B in the pictures.

A

B

2. Hold the pack in your left hand as your right hand takes about half the cards off from the bottom.

A

B

3. Bring the bottom half toward your body and then over the cards in your left hand and place it down on the table.

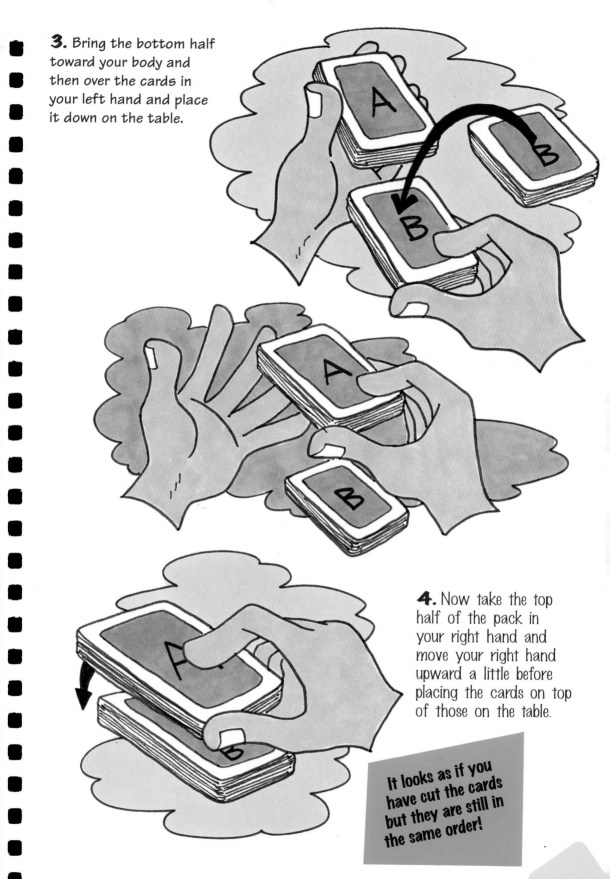

4. Now take the top half of the pack in your right hand and move your right hand upward a little before placing the cards on top of those on the table.

It looks as if you have cut the cards but they are still in the same order!

31

THE SPREAD

In many tricks you will need to show all the cards at the same time. A good way of doing this is to spread the cards out evenly on the table.

1. Place the pack on the table (which should have a cloth on it for best results).

2. Put your right hand flat on top of the pack with your fingers extending beyond the edge of the cards.

3. Press downward a little and move your hand to the right. The cards will spread out from the bottom of the pack as you let them pass under your fingertips.

It is not difficult to do but it does require practice to get the knack and to get the cards evenly spaced. This sort of technical skill helps to give your whole routine a polished and confident look.

When you want to show a complete pack of cards, use the spread described on page 32 — but have the cards face down.

1. To show the faces of the cards, put your left forefinger under the card at the left end of the spread.

2. Raise the edge of the card up and then push it over so it is face up. This will, in turn, cause all the other cards to turn over as well.

Only do this turnover when the cards are evenly spread. If they are not even, the turnover movement will be disrupted.

FAN-TASTIC

1. Hold the pack in your left hand with your thumb touching the top card at the lower end of the pack.

2. Now place the right hand on the pack with the fingers at one end and the thumb at the other. Bend the cards over your left forefinger and move your right hand in a circular motion to the right allowing the cards to spring from your fingers as you move.

3. Keep moving your right hand until all the cards have spread into a fan shape.

Don't worry if the cards do not spread evenly when you first try this. You may even drop some or all of the cards, but keep practicing and eventually you will be able to make the fan without even thinking about it.

QUICK CHANGE

Sometimes it is useful to change the pack of cards you are using without anyone knowing. You could, for example, be using a trick pack and then do some tricks with an ordinary pack so no one will suspect that a trick pack was used.

Or perhaps you want to do a trick where the cards have to be in a special order so you change the pack you have been using for the one that has the prearranged cards in it.

1. Here is an easy way of making that change without anyone knowing. You are using one pack and the other one is in your pocket, your handbag, or your magic case.

2. Finish a trick and then simply put the pack away as if you have finished performing.

3. Suddenly you decide to do a few more tricks and you go back to your pocket (or wherever) for the pack — only you take out the *other* pack.

Provided the cards have the same back design and you do this quite normally, no one will suspect that you have changed packs.

MAD JACK CARD PACK

TOUCH THE ACES

This trickery relies on your **Miracle Cards**, (*Ssh! you know*, the ones with the tapered edges.) They're also called a **Stripped Deck**.

1. Show the pack of cards face up and remove the **4 Aces** (or a 5 card straight flush).

2. Turn these 4 cards, or the flush, end to end and replace them in the pack in separate places.

3. Shuffle the cards a few times and, on the last shuffle, feel along the sides of the pack to bring the four Aces or flush cards to the top of the pack.

4. Turn the top four Aces, or flush, over and, one by one, show that they are now altogether on top of the pack. Wow!

But hold the applause...there's more!

Again, your spectator chooses any card and remembers the picture and number.

1. You, the Magician, return the card to the pack by turning the card end to end first without looking at the face of the card.

2. You now split the pack of cards in two, half face up, half face down.

3. The cards are now shuffled and the audience can see that the cards are completely mixed, with some facing up, others facing down.

4. You feel down the sides of the pack and pull the cards out and place them, face down, on top of the pack. Place the cards onto the table, face down, and fan out to show the only card face upward is the chosen card.

Ta-da!

I CAN READ YOUR MIND

Ask someone to shuffle a pack of cards and then remove a few, say ten or so.

1. Take the chosen cards and fan them out with their faces toward a second spectator. Ask that person to think of any card he can see. Ask him to point at it "to let everyone else know which card has been chosen."

2. As soon as the spectator points to the card you know what it is — even though the backs are toward you. This is because you secretly use your left thumb to push up the bottom corner of the card so you can see the index.

3. Gather the cards together and put them back in the pack.

4. You now pretend to read the spectator's mind and tell them what card they are thinking of.

37

There are lots of different versions of this trick. This one is a classic and fairly easy to do.

1. Put the four aces face up in a row on the table. Turn each ace face down and then deal three more cards from the pack on top of each ace.

2. Gather up the four piles into one packet of sixteen cards in which every fourth card is an ace.

3. Deal four cards face down in a row.

4. Take the next card from the top of the packet and use it to point to the fourth card. Ask someone to turn that card over — just to prove it is an ace. As the spectator is turning the card over, casually replace the fifth card on the bottom of the packet. The audience will not notice this since they are looking at the ace on the table.

This is known to magicians as "misdirection." While the audience is looking at one thing, you are doing the secret move upon which the trick depends. Misdirection is an important secret of successful magic.

5. Now continue dealing the rest of the packet into four piles. The audience must believe that the fourth pile contains all the aces. In fact, only the bottom card is an ace. Take this out (being careful not to show the other cards) and place it face up on the fourth pile "to mark the aces."

6. You must now "force" a spectator to pick the third pile which contains one ordinary card and three aces. This technique is described on page 29.

7. When the spectator has "chosen" pile three, pull out the bottom card (taking care not to show the aces) and place it face up on top of the pile.

8. Now exchange the positions of the two face-up "marker" cards. Turn over the fourth pile — the aces have vanished!

9. When you turn over the "selected" pile the audience sees that the aces have arrived there.

DO AS I DO

This is another popular theme in magic and there are lots of different ways of doing it.

1. Shuffle the pack and cut it into two halves (it is actually more effective if you get a spectator to do this).

2. The spectator takes one half of the pack and you take the other half. Ask the spectator to do exactly the same as you do.

3. Fan the cards toward yourself, pick out any card, remember it, and place it on top of your half. In fact, you do not take any notice of the card you remove. All you really do is memorize the bottom card.

40

4. Place the two halves of the pack together, making sure that your half goes on top of the spectator's half. Give the pack a few cuts.

5. State that you are going to use your magic powers to make the cards come together. You name your card (actually the one you saw at the bottom of your half) and the spectator names the card he chose.

6. When the cards are spread out face up on the table, the two cards are found to be next to one another. Miracle of miracles!

41

M E N T A L

Before you start this trick you need to have three cards in your pocket.

1. Ask a spectator to take any four cards from the pack. Show the four cards to another spectator and ask her to think of any one. You must remember the four cards and the order they are in.

2. When the spectator has made a mental selection, place the four cards in your pocket behind the three cards already there.

3. Take the three "extra" cards from your pocket, one at a time, and place them on the pack. Do this in a mysterious manner as though it requires great concentration. The audience thinks you have only one card left, but, in fact, you still have all four.

4. Ask the spectator to name the mentally selected card. Since you know the order of the four cards, you can instantly locate the right one and bring it from your pocket — ample proof that you are telepathic!

Although the trick is over, you still have three cards left in your pocket. They can be secretly returned to the pack later or used for another performance of the trick (you won't get away with it more than twice, though).

An easy way to get the cards back in the pack is to simply place the whole pack in your pocket when you have finished the trick.

ODD MAN OUT

Before your show, divide the pack into reds and blacks. Reassemble the pack with the black cards on the top and the red cards on the bottom. You are now ready to show the trick.

1. Invite someone to pick a card. Fan only the upper half of the pack face down, so that the spectator takes a black card. Close the fan and ask the person to remember the card.

2. Fan the bottom half of the pack face down for the return of the card. The black card is thus replaced among the red cards (although the audience does not know about this, of course).

3. Give the pack a few false cuts "to lose the chosen card" (this will not disturb the secret arrangement of the cards).

4. Now casually look through the pack as you say that you are going to read the person's mind. Among the red cards will be one black card — the spectator's card. Make a mental note of this card.

5. Give the pack a good shuffle, thus destroying any evidence as to how the trick was done!

6. Ask the spectator to concentrate on the card and you read their mind by naming the card you saw. Distribute smelling salts as required...

SORT THEM OUT

This trick requires some secret preparation. Take seven black cards and seven red cards and put them, face up, on top of one another in this order: red, black, black, red, red, black, black, red, red, black, black, black, red, red.

1. Turn the cards over and put them on top of the rest of the pack and you are ready.

1, 2, 3, 4, 5...

2. Say that you are going to do a trick with just a few cards. As you are speaking, silently count off eleven cards, in order, from the top of the pack. Bunch the cards together so no one can see how many cards you have taken.

3. Keep this packet of cards in your hands and put the rest of the pack down on the table.

4. Take the two top cards from the packet in your hands and turn them over to show you have a red and a black card. Replace these cards on the bottom of the packet you are holding. Now show the next pair of cards (one red, one black) and place them on the bottom. Continue showing pairs of cards until you have shown six pairs in all.

5. The last pair is not placed beneath the packet but put on the table face up. These will be your "marker" cards. Drop the packet of cards back on top of the pack.

6. Take two cards from the top of the pack and mix them up face down. Ask someone to point to whichever card they think is the black card of the pair. The chosen card is put face down on top of the black marker, the other one is placed face down to one side.

7. Take the next pair from the top of the pack, mix them up and say: "Which do you think is the red card this time?" Put the chosen card on the red marker and discard the other one.

8. Do the same with the next pair, asking which is the black and placing the chosen card on the black marker.

9. For the following pair, the spectator has to choose which is red and this choice goes on the red marker. Do the same on the next turn, but with the blacks. For the final pair, the spectator has to choose which is red and this card goes on the red marker.

10. Casually pick up the discarded cards and drop them on the pack as you move the pack to one side.

11. Emphasize the fact that the spectator had a "free choice" every time. Now turn over the three cards on the red marker – they are all red. And the three cards on the black marker are all black!

If you follow the instructions carefully, this trick works itself but you should practice it in private first until you are sure you are doing it right.

ADVANCE

1. Have the cards shuffled and returned to you. Spread the cards with their faces toward you as you say: "I am going to predict something that will happen in the future." As you say this, look for the ninth card from the top of the pack. Let us say, for example, that it is the Four of Clubs.

2. Put the cards down on the table as you pick up a pencil and a piece of paper. Write on the paper (being careful not to let anyone see what you are writing): "I think you will choose the Four of Clubs (or whatever the ninth card was)." Fold the paper in two and put it on the table.

3. Now ask someone to give you any number from 10 to 19. Whatever number they choose, you count that number of cards off from the top of the pack, one at a time, and place them to one side.

4. You then announce that the chosen number is made up of two digits and that you will add them together. So, for example, if the chosen number was 17, the 1 and 7 added together will give you 8. You then count that number of cards (e.g. 8), again one at a time, from the top of the *small* pack and back onto the *big* pack.

5. The card now on top of the small pack seems to have been chosen at random. Ask someone to turn that card over and then read your prediction. You are – surprise, surprise – absolutely correct!

This trick works because the digits of any number between 10 and 19, when added together and deducted from the chosen number, will always result in 9.

Since the card you predicted was the ninth card from the top of the pack, you will always be right.

THE FIFTH CARD

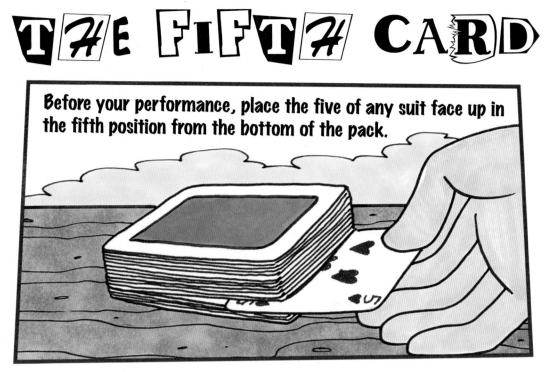

Before your performance, place the five of any suit face up in the fifth position from the bottom of the pack.

1. Fan the cards for someone to pick one, but be careful not to expose the reversed card. Ask the spectator to look at his card and remember it. Ask the spectator to show the card to the rest of the audience, too.

2. Have the chosen card replaced on the bottom of the pack.

3. Cut the pack, burying the card somewhere in the middle of the pack. In fact, cut the pack a few more times so the card is completely lost.

4. Say that you are going to make one card turn over and that card will help you find the chosen card. Spread the cards face down across the table until the reversed card becomes visible. The fifth card to the left of the five is the spectator's card.

Nine cards are laid face up on the table. While you are out of the room, a member of the audience points to any one of the cards. When you return to the room, you immediately name the card that was pointed at.

1. First, the nine cards have to be laid out on the table in three rows of three. You also need the help of a friend with a poker face who casually holds the remainder of the pack while secretly signaling to you which card has been chosen.

2. To do this, you must both imagine the top card of the casually held pack is divided into nine sections, corresponding to the nine cards on the table.

3. Your friend simply puts his thumb on the appropriate section.

A quick glance at his hands as you enter the room tells you the position of the chosen card.

It is as simple as that. Really overact the part of a genuine mind reader and your friends may actually believe that you have special powers!

THOUGHT TRANSMISSION

TURNOVER

Before showing this trick, secretly turn the bottom card of the pack face up.

1. Spread the cards face down (being careful not to show the bottom card) and ask someone to take out any card.

2. You now ask them to show the card around so everyone can see it. As you say this you transfer the pack from one hand to the other and turn it over at the same time. Do NOT look at your hands as you do this or you will give the trick away...

TRICKERY

3. The spectator now pushes the chosen card face down into the face down pack (it looks as if the pack is face down but, in actual fact, all the cards are face up except for the top card). Keep a firm hold on the pack as the chosen card is returned so no one will see that the cards are really face up.

4. Now take the pack behind your back as you say that you are going to find the chosen card and that you will turn it over in the pack. All you actually do behind your back is take off the reversed card, turn it over, and push it into the pack.

5. You then turn the whole pack over as you bring it forward and place it on the table. Ask the spectator for the name of the chosen card and then spread the cards across the table. All the cards are face down except one, and that is the chosen card!

Before starting this trick, you must know the top card of the pack. You can find this out by looking through the pack to remove the jokers – at the same time secretly taking a look at the top card.

1. Give the cards a shuffle as described on pages 24-25 (this keeps the noted card on the top).

2. Place the cards on your outstretched palm, cut off about half the cards, and place the top half on your fingers.

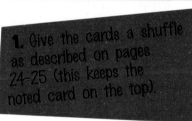

3. Ask a spectator to look at the top card of the half nearest to him (the half on your fingers) and you look at the top card of the other half (if you want to repeat the trick you will need to remember this card – if not you do not have to pay attention to it).

4. Now place your half of the pack on top of the other half. You now tell everyone the card you looked at (at least that is what you say). What you *really* do is name the partner of the card you remembered earlier — so if the card was the Seven of Spades you say "Seven of Clubs." Everyone will be amazed when the spectator announces the card he saw (in this example it will be the Seven of Spades).

5. You are now ready to repeat the trick (using the card you really saw). So, if you saw the Nine of Diamonds for example, this will now be the top card of the pack. When you announce the card you "saw" on your half of the pack, you say "Nine of Hearts."

You can now repeat this trick several times, but I wouldn't advise doing it more than three times or your audience may get suspicious!

SPECTATOR POWER

Before performing the trick, you must secretly put the four aces on the top of the pack.

1. Place the pack on the table and ask someone to cut it into two piles. You must keep track of which pile the aces are on.

2. Now ask that both of the two piles be cut in half, also. You will now have four piles of cards on the table. The aces will be on one of the end piles so make sure you keep track of them in your mind.

3. Point to the pile at the opposite end of the row to the aces and ask someone to take off three cards. Put these cards at the bottom of the pile and then ask them to deal the top three cards, one at a time, onto each of the other three piles.

4. Ask the spectator to do the same with the other three piles in sequence, making sure that the last pile to be dealt with is the one that has the aces.

The top card of each pile is now turned over to reveal...the four aces!

You'll need a little behind-the-scenes preparation here: put the four sevens on top of the pack; on top of the sevens, place a four, then a two and then an ace; put seven cards on top of these.

YOU WILL CHOOSE THE SEVEN PILE!

1. O.K. — you're ready to perform. Write on a piece of paper "You will choose the seven pile." Do not let anyone see what you have written. Fold the paper and place it on the table.

2. Take the "ready-prepared" pack and deal off seven cards into one pile, three cards into a second pile, and four cards into a third pile.

3. Get someone to pick any one of the three piles. Make it perfectly clear that they have a free choice of pile — they can even change their mind if they wish.

SEVEN CARDS

ADDS UP TO SEVEN

FOUR SEVENS

YOU WILL CHOOSE THE SEVEN PILE!

4. You now open the paper and show what you wrote earlier.

5a. If the first pile was chosen, you simply count the number of cards in it — there are seven cards so your prediction is correct.

5b. If the second pile was chosen, turn the three cards over and add the numbers on each card together — four plus two, plus one makes seven — so, again, your prediction is correct.

5c. If the last pile was chosen, turn over the cards to reveal the four sevens.

So, whichever pile is chosen, your prediction seems to be correct. Obviously, don't let anyone see the contents of the unchosen piles or your trickery will be exposed!

57

THAT'S

1. From a shuffled pack, take out three groups of seven cards. Do not count the cards out, try to make it look as if you are just taking out bunches of cards at random.

2. Ask a member of the audience to point to one of the three piles. Fan the cards of that pile toward your volunteer and ask him to think of any card. It is a good idea to turn your head away while he points to the card, so that some of the other spectators will know what it is just in case he should forget — you'd be surprised!

3. Close the fan and place this pile of cards between the other two. Deal the cards out into three separate piles.

MAGIC

4. Now pick up each pile in turn and ask if the chosen card is visible. Whichever pile holds the chosen card is then placed between the other two. Once again the cards are dealt out into three piles.

5. Again ask which of the three piles contains the chosen card and place this pile between the other two.

6. Claim: "I think you'll agree that the cards are now well mixed and since you are only *thinking* of a card, there is no way I could know where your card is." The spectator will have to agree with this, so you continue: "Whenever I do this trick, everyone says to me 'That's magic!' so I'll use that expression to find your card."

7. You then take one card from the top of the pile for each letter of T-H-A-T-S-M-A-G-I-C. Ask for the name of the chosen card. Turn over the next one and it will be the very same card!

1. Have a card chosen, remembered, and returned to the pack, as described on page 21.

2. Flick through the pack from the bottom. When you find the chosen card, do not stop there by revealing it. Starting on the chosen card, run through the pack above moving one card for each letter of the name — so, if the chosen card was the Six of Clubs you would be moving the cards as you say to yourself S-I-X-O-F-C-L-U-B-S.

3. Look at the card you have reached and spell that card to yourself, again starting on this card, move one card for each letter. Let us assume that this card is the Queen of Hearts, so you spell Q-U-E-E-N-O-F-H-E-A-R-T-S.

4. Cut the pack at that point so the card you reached on the "S" is now the top card of the pack.

5. If by any chance you reach the top of the pack during this operation, simply continue spelling from the bottom.

6. Say you cannot find the chosen card so you will have to use some stronger magic. Tell the spectator that you want him to spell his card, taking one card for each letter from the top of the pack. To show him what to do you say: "If, for example, you chose the Queen of Hearts (or whichever card you spotted in no.3) you'd spell one card for each letter like this, Q-U-E-E-N-O-F-H-E-A-R-T-S." Imagine everyone's surprise when the card you turn over at the end really is the Queen of Hearts.

There will be an even greater surprise when the spectator then spells his card!

KARATE CHOP

1. Have a card chosen, remembered, and then placed back on top of the pack. Do the shuffle control described on page 24. It seems that the card has been shuffled in the pack but it is really still on the top.

2. Hold the pack face up in your right hand, with your right thumb on the face card and all your fingers under the pack.

3. Now ask someone to give a straight downward karate-type chop at the pack of cards to knock them all out of your hand and onto the floor.

4. If you keep a firm grip on the pack, all the cards will fall to the floor except the chosen one which remains face up between finger and thumb — the spectator has found his own card with his karate magic.

1. Go into a photo booth and get four pictures of yourself. For each picture hold a playing card near your face (have four different cards – one for each photograph).

2. Put one photograph in an envelope and save the others for another day.

3. Hand the envelope to someone and then get them to pick a card. In actual fact, you force the card that is on the photograph in the envelope. The force on page **28** is quite good for this trick.

4. When the card has been chosen, ask the spectator to open the envelope. Inside, there is a photograph of you holding up the very card that has been selected!

PHOTO PREDICTION

TELEPHONE TELEPATHY

A card is chosen and you then call your friend who you say is a fellow "master magician." The magician tells the spectator the name of the chosen card.

1. How? Well, first you must discover the identity of the chosen card. "Your Card" on page 26 tells you how to do this.

2. You now say you are going to telephone this magician friend of yours. When the telephone is answered, you say: "May I talk to the magician, please?" That is your code to let your friend know you are doing this trick. Immediately, he says: "Clubs, hearts, spades, diamonds." You stop him on the right suit by saying, "Yes, please."

3. He now starts counting: "Ace, Two, Three, Four ...". When he reaches the correct number, you say: "Hang on, I have a call for you," and you hand the telephone to the spectator who chose the card.

4. The magician on the other end of the line then tells the spectator what card he chose!